Hide and Seek

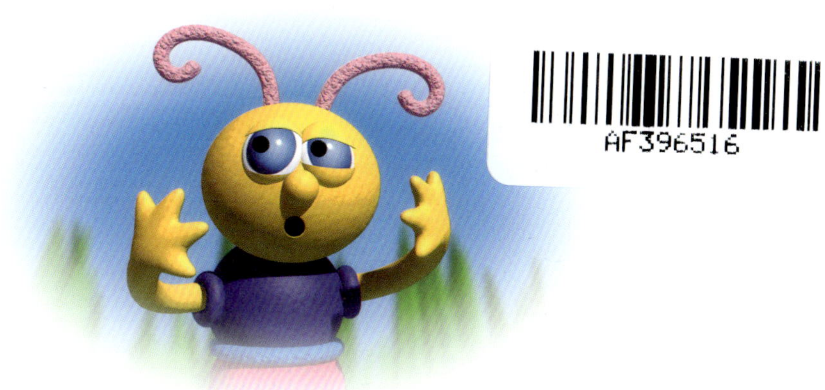

Tony Mitton

Illustrated by Andy Parker

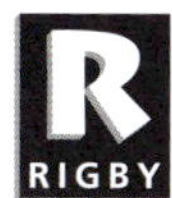

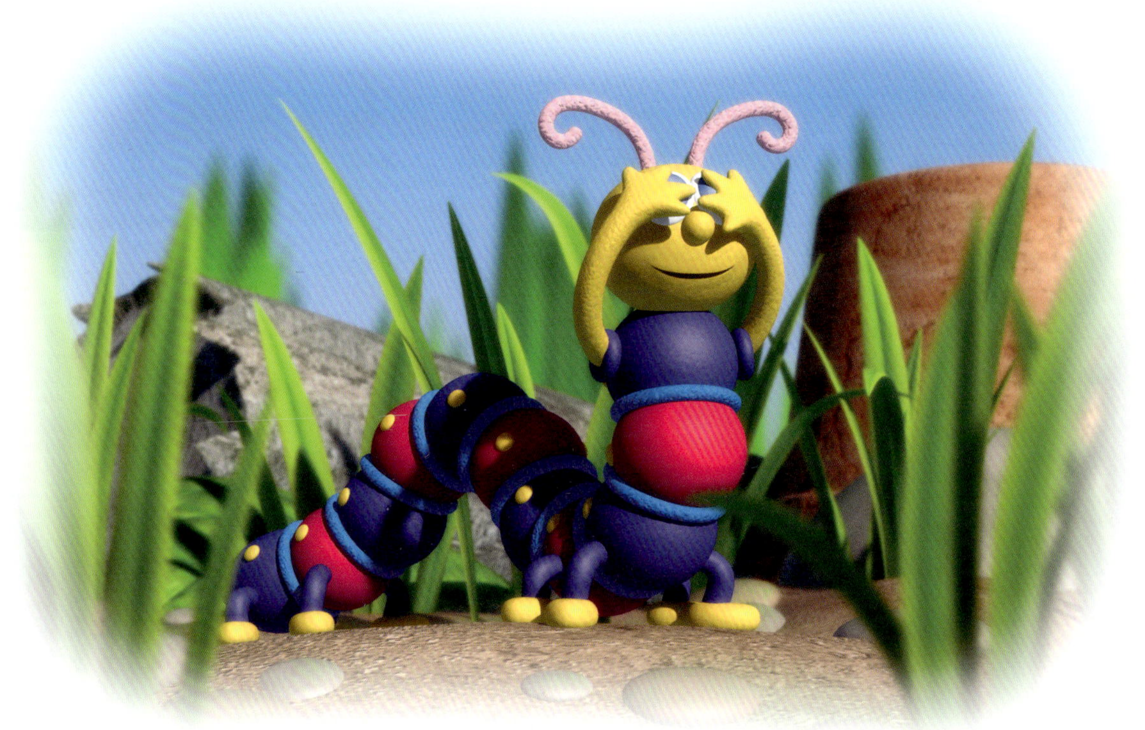

one curly caterpillar

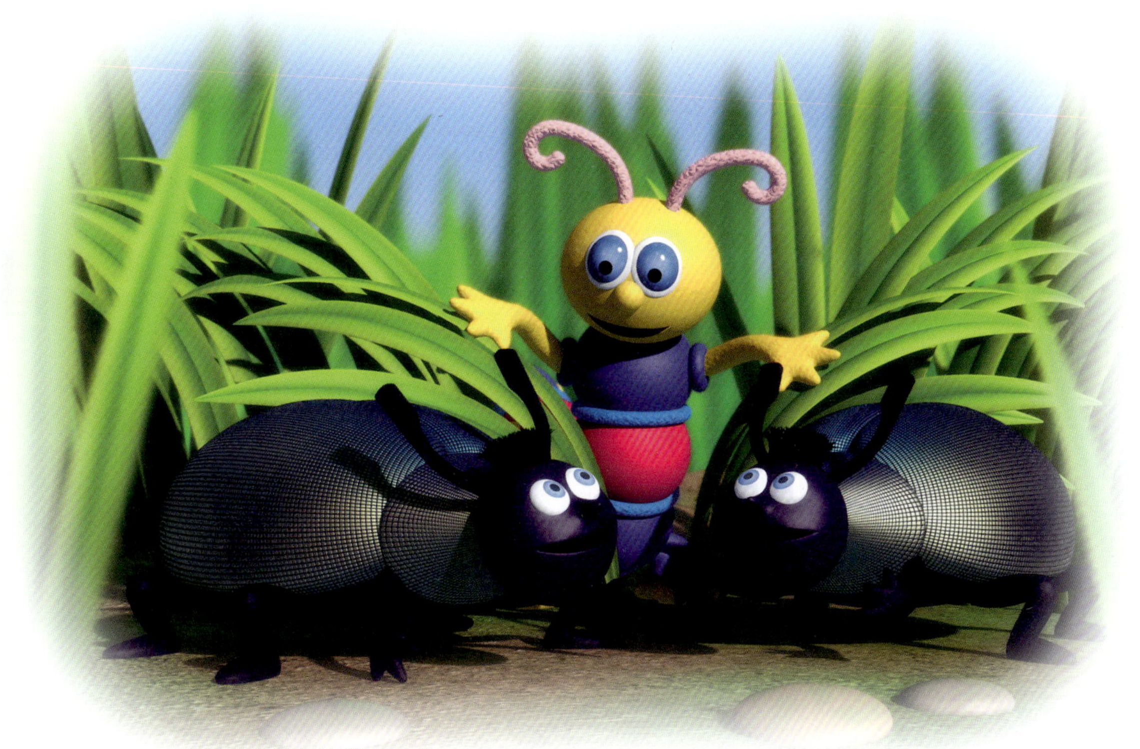

two big beetles

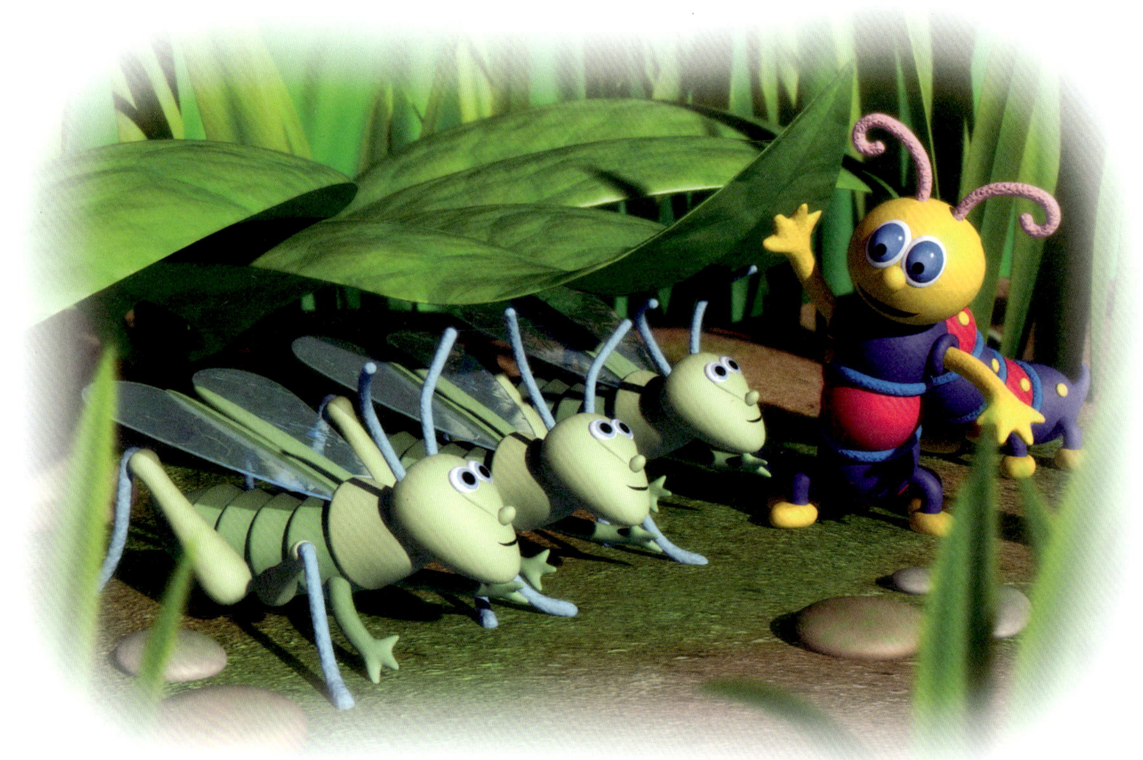

three green grasshoppers

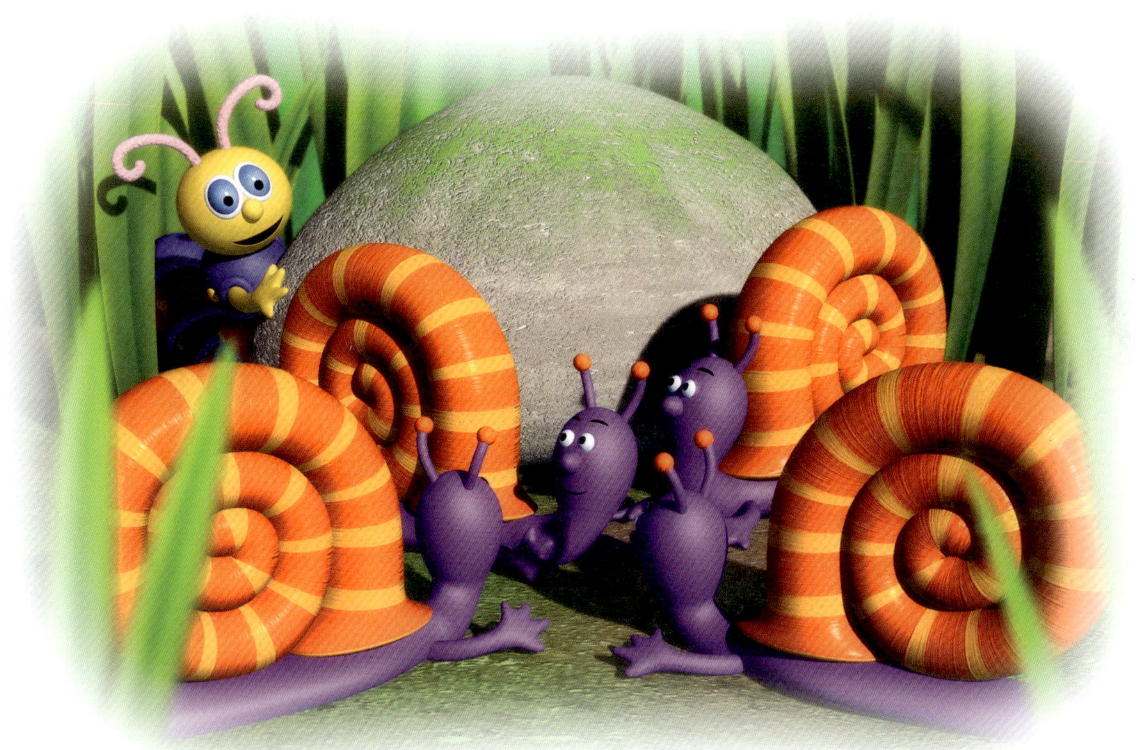

four slippery snails

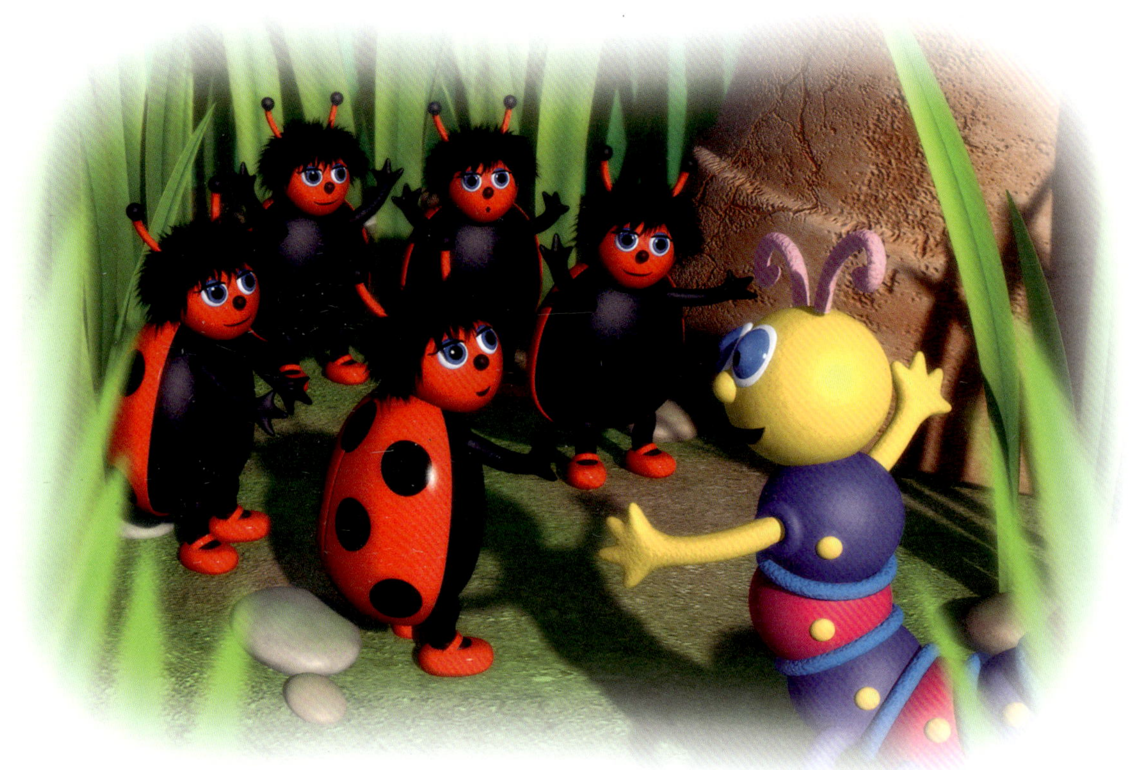

five little ladybirds

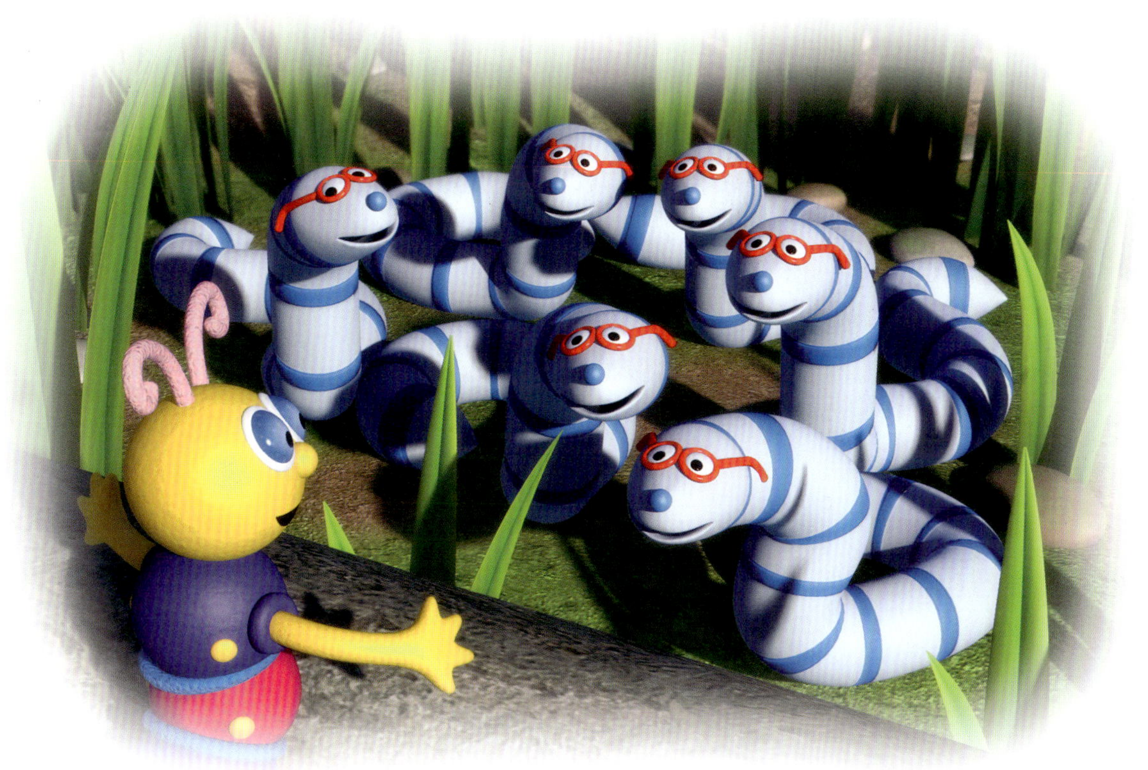

six wiggly worms

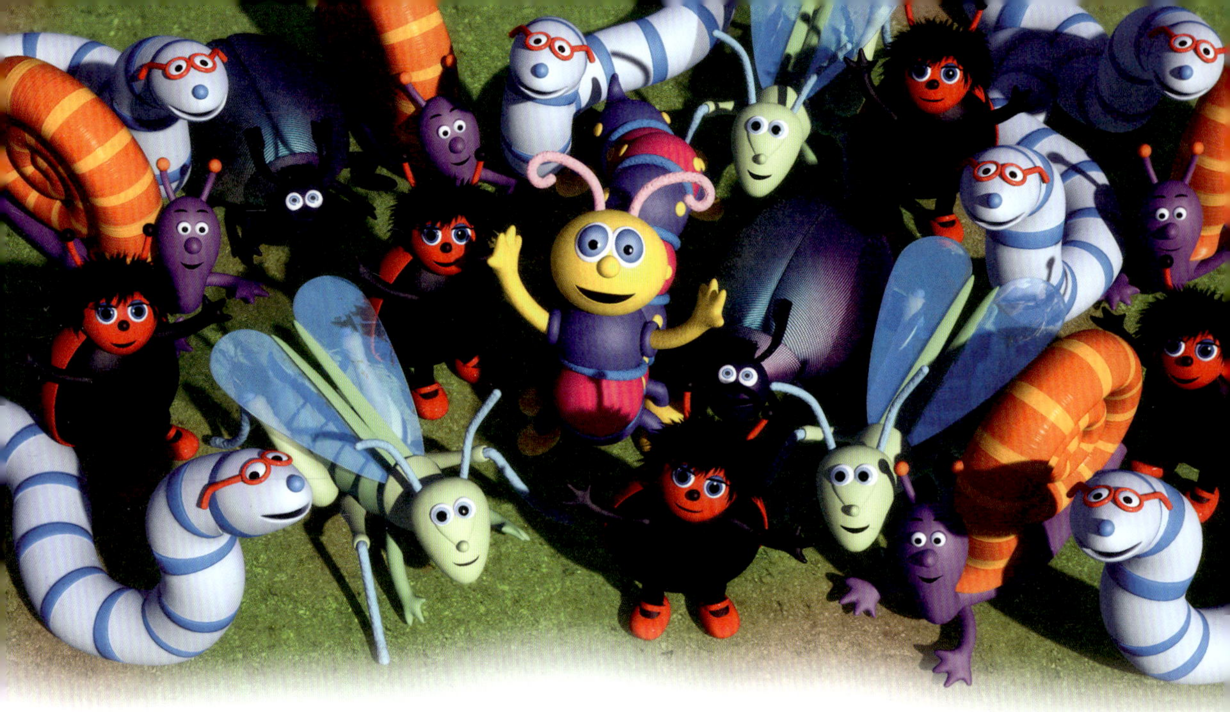

lots of laughing

little friends

8